SOMEBODY FAMOUS

By
D. M. Larson

Copyright © 2005
All Rights Reserved*

*For permission to perform this script, contact
doug@freedrama.net

Cast of Characters (5w 2m)

DONNA – Prisoner who is a computer hacker with a plan to escape

MACY – Ditzy prisoner who loves jewelry and loves GUS

REGGIE – Wise-cracking prisoner who loves a good scam

GUS – Bumbling guard who likes MACY

MELINDA – Famous actress who is in jail for murder

CAPTAIN – Tough guard who bosses everyone around

12006 – Quiet prisoner who prefers to go by her number rather than name

Time and Place
A present day old theatre in New Mexico.

ACT 1

(Lights come up on an old theatre that has seen better days. The stage is littered with junk and debris. It looks as if a play had a closing night and everything was left to rot and never put away. Three women in yellow jumpers enter with cleaning supplies [MACY, DONNA, and 12006]. They are followed by two security guards [CAPTAIN and GUS].)

CAPTAIN
Welcome to your tour of duty, ladies.

DONNA
Wow, Captain. You know how to pick 'em.

MACY
What is this place anyway?

GUS
It's a theatre.

MACY
A theater? But where's the movie screen? And the popcorn.

GUS
I like popcorn.

CAPTAIN
It's not that kind of theatre you idiots. It's a play theatre.

MACY
Play theatre? Where they play what?

CAPTAIN
Oh, forget it.

DONNA
Don't worry, Captain. I'll explain it to her.

CAPTAIN
Don't bother. Just get to work.

DONNA
So what are we supposed to do?

CAPTAIN
Clean the place.

DONNA
What for?

CAPTAIN
So Macy can play.

MACY
Really?

CAPTAIN
No! Now get to work.
(Heads off)
Watch 'em, Gus. Gotta take a pee.

GUS
Yes, sir. I got my eye on them.

(Follows CAPTAIN off)

CAPTAIN
(Off)
Get back in there.

GUS
(Re-enters)
Yes, sir, Captain.

MACY
What a grouch.

GUS
Sorry about that. He gets that way when he doesn't get his donuts.

MACY
What happened to his donuts?

GUS
I don't know. I bought him a couple like always and set them up in the front seat and after I loaded you all up they were gone.

DONNA
(Sees 12006 and REGGIE eating something)
Gee, wonder where they went.

GUS
(Sees 12006 with a mouthful)
What have you got in your mouth?
(12006 ignores him)
I'm talking to you prisoner.
(To MACY)
What's her name again?

MACY
We don't know.

GUS
You don't know? What do you call her?

DONNA
She likes to be called by her number.

GUS
You mean 12006?

DONNA
That's right.

GUS
That has to the stupidest...
(Turns and 12006 is in his face)
...thing I've ever said.
(12006 goes back to her cleaning)
Can't we call her 6 for short?
(12006 gives him a dirty look)
Guess not.

MACY
(Trying to be friendly to 12006)
How about 006? Just like James Bond.
(12006 gives her a really dirty look)
Actually I love the sound of 12006. Rolls right off the tounge. Just like Tiffany. I love that name.

(12006 rolls her eyes and goes back to cleaning)

GUS
Tiffany is a pretty name. Maybe I'll name my first daughter that.

MACY
(Pouty)
You having a baby with someone?

GUS
No. I'm not even dating now.

MACY
(Smiles)
Really?

GUS
I just haven't met the right lady yet I guess. Momma says some lady will see how special I am one day.

MACY
I think you're special, Gus.

DONNA
We all think you're special.

(12006 smiles at this)

MACY
Maybe the right lady is right before your eyes and you don't even know.

GUS
(Looks at MACY longingly and she returns his gaze)
Maybe…

REGGIE
Wow, that was sweeter than those donuts.

DONNA
If you guys want to get a room, I'll keep an eye on things here.

GUS
(Gets all official)
I have no clue what you're talking about.

MACY
(Hurt)
You don't?

DONNA
I thought you guys were about to pick out china patterns.

REGGIE
I thought they were about to get busy!
(12006 smiles)

GUS
Back to work… or… or…

REGGIE
Or what?

GUS
I'll go get the captain.

MACY
Leave Gus alone. He's nice.

REGGIE
He'd like to be real nice to you.
(GUS is uneasy)
He's blushing. Ha! I guess they think we must be pretty lightweight if they send Gus to watch us.

DONNA
I know the three of us are. But how do you explain 12006?

MACY
What's she in for?

REGGIE
Come on. We're all innocent. You know that.

MACY
I wish I was innocent.

REGGIE
So what did you do?

MACY
Shoplifting.

REGGIE
Shoplifting. That's it?

DONNA
When you take a five finger discount on jewelry it's a bit more serious.

REGGIE
What did you steal?

DONNA
She got caught with enough jewelry to open her own store.

MACY
I'm sorry but I like pretty things.

REGGIE
So if I wave something shiny will you chase it?

MACY
(After a moment)
Maybe.

REGGIE
I had a cat like that once. Hey, is that where they get that word cat-burgler?

(MACY starts sweeping and cleaning with 12006)

DONNA
Don't know. I'd google it if they'd let us use the internet.

(Directs last part at GUS)

GUS
You're not allowed near anything like a computer.

DONNA
I can't even get near a phone.

REGGIE
Why not?

DONNA
I'm in for hacking.

REGGIE
Hacking?

DONNA
Computer hacking.

REGGIE
Why can't you get near a phone?

DONNA
I cost MCI a whole lot of money and they got the judge to do that. I think I'm the reason they went bankrupt a few years back.

GUS
More work and less talk.

REGGIE
Hey, my break ain't over yet.

GUS
You can't have a break until you start working.

REGGIE
(Pushes her broom a few times and then stops again)
How's that?

GUS
You want me to get the Captain?

REGGIE
I wouldn't if I was you. Remember last time you called him out of that adult bookstore down the street. He was pissed.

GUS
(Nervous)
He was, wasn't he?

MACY
Don't worry, Gus. We'll work.

(MACY cleans as does DONNA)

DONNA
(While working)
So Reggie. What you in for?
(REGGIE ignores her and starts cleaning for the first time)
Sorry... what you falsely accused of?

REGGIE
They say I was passing around stolen checks but I don't think they had enough evidence to convict.

DONNA
And what about 12006?

REGGIE
Who knows?

MACY
She's not in red so she didn't kill anybody...

(12006 gives MACY a dirty look)

REGGIE
...yet.

(MACY moves and cleans closer to GUS)

MACY
So why are we cleaning this theatre?

GUS
Warden got this special funding for what he calls Drama Therapy from the state arts council.

REGGIE
Drama therapy? Where's the drama in this?

DONNA
Are we going to do anything besides clean this place?

GUS
Not that I know of. I saw two contracts. One with money for drama therapy and the other for cleaning up this theatre for the city.

DONNA
So the warden gets money from the arts council and then gets money again from the city. The city gets a cleaned up theatre and we supposedly get something out of it too.

REGGIE
Wait. I've heard of drama therapy and that's acting and stuff. This ain't acting. GUS Sorry, that's all I know.

MACY
Maybe if we whistle why we work. Or sing... (Dances and sings with her broom) "Chim-chimminy, chim-chimminy, chim, chim..." (MACY runs into 12006) Or not.

REGGIE
So basically the warden is ripping off the state arts council.

GUS
Oh, he wouldn't do that.

MACY
Maybe he's got some kind of idea for us after we clean this up. Maybe we'll do a play.

REGGIE
I vote for Oh, Calcutta.

(12006 smiles at this idea)

DONNA
So where did the warden get this brilliant idea of his?

GUS
Well, the rumor...
(Looks around)

DONNA
It's okay, Gus. The captain's not that quick of a reader.

REGGIE
And the man enjoys his dirty novels very much.

GUS
I shouldn't be telling you guys nothing.

(GUS turns away and DONNA pushes MACY over to him)

MACY
Please, Gus. Could you maybe tell us a little what you heard?

GUS
Well, I'll tell you, Macy.

(Others pretend to work but are moving closer and closer to GUS)

MACY
So what'd you hear?

GUS
I heard that the warden is doing this to get a little media attention. See, we got a new inmate coming. Somebody famous.

MACY
Famous? Who?

GUS
Melinda Street.

REGGIE
Melinda Street!

GUS
I shouldn't have said anything.

REGGIE
She's like uber-famous.

GUS
Please don't tell anyone I told you.

REGGIE
And what do I get for keeping my mouth shut?

GUS
(Looks around nervously)
What do you want?

REGGIE
You know that Mickey D's around the corner?

GUS
Oh, no.

REGGIE
(Sings or raps)
I want "two all meat patties special dressing if you please with an extra large fry on the side."

DONNA
I'm not sure that's how that jingle goes.

REGGIE
Whatever... you get the idea.

GUS I can't leave you all alone. If the captain found out...

MACY
Don't worry, Gus. We won't go anywhere. We're yellow shirts. We're not dangerous.

GUS
Fine. I'm going.

(GUS exits and REGGIE shouts after him)

REGGIE
And I want diet Cola. I'm trying to watch my figure.

MACY
He's so sweet.

REGGIE
And he's got it for you bad. He'd do anything you asked him. We've got such a sweet deal on this job. Today burgers. Tomorrow pizza.

MACY
Please don't ask him to do too much. I don't want him to get fired.

REGGIE
Fine, we'll order out for Chinese then.

DONNA
Melinda Street. She's coming here? Didn't she win an academy award?

MACY
Two. For "The Guns of Lincoln County" and "The English Patient's Woman."
(MACY's voice gets so excited it's almost a scream) I'm like her biggest fan.

REGGIE
Just don't go all Kathy Bates on us, okay?

DONNA
I wonder what she's in for?

REGGIE
Here comes Gus. Maybe he can tell us.

(GUS rushes back in)

REGGIE
Where's my burger?

GUS
I nearly ran into the Captain. He's coming.

REGGIE
I guess we'll just have to tell him about what you said about Ms. Street then.

GUS
Please don't. Macy? Please.

MACY
Come on, Reggie. Gus tried to get your burger.

DONNA
Hey, what if he tells us what she's in for? I'm dying to know.

REGGIE
Okay, fine. Spill it, Gus.

GUS
If I tell you then you won't say anything to the Captain.

REGGIE
Cross my heart and hope you die.

MACY
Thanks, Reggie. Okay, Gussy. Please tell us.

GUS
Fine. She's a red shirt. She's in for murder.

MACY
Murder? No!

GUS
She was in this murder mystery on Broadway and she killed the entire cast.

DONNA
Everyone? For real?

GUS
For real. And nobody knew it until the play was over. I mean like all the actors were supposed to pretend to die but she really was killing them.

MACY
I can't believe it.

DONNA
Do they know why she did it?

GUS
Nope.

REGGIE
Couldn't she go for an insanity plea? She sounds like she went nuts to me.

GUS
She was calm and collected in the trial. And she checked out fine on all the tests for mental stability.

MACY
Come to think of it, there have been some other mysterious deaths during her career. Boating accidents, fouled up stunts...

REGGIE
Wild. How come she didn't get off like OJ and Michael?

DONNA
She's a woman that's why.

REGGIE
I knew it had to be something like that. Just like Martha Stewart. I don't see no Donald Trump in jail but my girl M. Diddy was in clink in no time.

MACY
You know Martha Stewart?

REGGIE
We did a little time together.

MACY
I loved her show.

REGGIE
I taught her how to make a switchblade out of a paring knife. Maybe she'll have that on one of her shows!

(12006 smiles at this)

DONNA
So we're cleaning this theatre up for Melinda's revival of her play? I'm not acting in that. Might be therapeutic for her but not for me.

MACY
I would love to act with Melinda Street. It would be like a dream come true.

REGGIE
Even if it means she cuts your throat?

MACY
(Thinks a moment)
Maybe.

GUS
Don't worry, Macy. I wouldn't let anything happen to you.

REGGIE
Ah, Gus. You're a real American hero.

MACY
Isn't he though?

GUS
Oh, Macy.

REGGIE
Where is that captain? Were you making that up so you didn't have to get my combo meal?

(MACY screams and points off. Everyone jumps)

REGGIE
What was that for?

MACY
It's... it's...

DONNA
Melinda Street.
(CAPTAIN enters with MELINDA who is in a red prison jumper but has accessorized with jewelry and hair stuff)

CAPTAIN
Let me introduce you to the girls.

MELINDA
If I must...

CAPTAIN
You all are going to be spending a lot of time together here. Might as well get on friendly terms.

MELINDA
(Sarcastic)
Oh, yes. Let's all be friends.

CAPTAIN
This here is Macy Jensen.

MELINDA
Macy? Where'd you ever get a name like that?

MACY
I was conceived in a Macy's department store.

MELINDA
Why does this not surprise me? I suppose you were raised in a trailer too.

MACY
Nice jewelry.

(MACY touches MELINDA's hand)

CAPTAIN
Hands off.

(GUS uses this as an excuse to grab MACY)

MELINDA
How dare you grab me like that!

CAPTAIN
You okay, Ms. Street?

MELINDA
Yes, you can let go of me now.

(MACY shows her newly acquired ring to REGGIE)

GUS
(Pulls MACY aside)
You've got to give that back.

MACY
But it's so pretty, Gussy. Like a wedding ring.

(GUS blushes)

CAPTAIN
Gus, what are you doing?

MACY
Just getting handle on me.

REGGIE
I'll bet he is.

CAPTAIN
Our priority is to provide protection for Ms. Street. Got it?

MACY
That's what he was doing. I was getting way too close for comfort.

REGGIE
And now Gus is checking her perimeter.

CAPTAIN
Shut up, you.

DONNA
So what's the warden got planned for us?

CAPTAIN
Drama therapy that's what. We're going to restore this theatre and then put on a play.

MELINDA
You have got to be kidding. A play? With this crew?

MACY
I did a play once in high school.

MELINDA
Well, that just makes you a superstar then. Let's cast her as the lead.

MACY
Really?

MELINDA
Idiot.

DONNA
I'm not sure this is going to work.

MELINDA
The voice of reason at last.

(MACY is all hurt and GUS goes to comfort her and they slowly slip out during the following)

CAPTAIN
Well, you're gonna make it work. The warden got the money for this project and he's not giving the money back. And with a big name like Ms. Street involved, this will bring a lot of much needed media attention for the warden.

DONNA
Media attention? What for?

CAPTAIN
The warden is publishing a book and we hope to have this little play ready for the day it hits the bookstores.

REGGIE
The warden wrote a book?

CAPTAIN
He had some writer come in and help him but it's his book.

REGGIE
What's it about?

CAPTAIN
His plan for reforming the entire prison system in our country.

REGGIE
What's it called? The Idiot's Guide to being a Warden?

(12006 smiles)

CAPTAIN
Cute.

MELINDA
He gave me an advance copy. It's called "More Prisons Today, A Better World Tomorrow."

REGGIE
Oh, puke.

DONNA
Yes, that's solution. Lock everyone up and the world will be a better place.

CAPTAIN
I got a better title. More Executions Today, A Better Day for Me.

DONNA
Not very catchy.

CAPTAIN
But it would solve all the problems pretty quick. Kill 'em all and let God sort them out.

REGGIE
That's real Christian of you.

DONNA
Actually I read that it costs more to execute a criminal than it does to keep them locked up.

CAPTAIN
Liberal propaganda I'm sure.

DONNA
In fact, I'll bet if they focused on reforming people before they got to prison, they wouldn't need so many of them.

CAPTAIN
You voted for Clinton didn't you?

DONNA
8 or 9 times I think. Vote early and often is what I say.

CAPTAIN
You hacked a voting machine? You know how illegal that is?

DONNA
No, wait. I'm innocent. Nearly forgot.

REGGIE
Nice save.

DONNA
But it was in Florida so is it still illegal?

REGGIE
Only if you're a democrat.

MELINDA
Well, all this chit-chat has been a blast, but it's almost time for my massage...

CAPTAIN
Oh, right... let's go.

REGGIE
What?! I think I want to be a red shirt now.

CAPTAIN
Ms. Street has special arrangements.

REGGIE
Who's giving her the massage? The warden?

MELINDA
I have my own private masseuse, thank you.

REGGIE
(Mocking)
"I have my own private masseuse, thank you."

CAPTAIN
Back to work, ladies. Let's make this place pretty for Ms. Street's play.

(CAPTAIN and MELINDA start to go, but DONNA stops them)

DONNA
So what play are we doing?

CAPTAIN
I don't know. Did the warden say, Ms. Street?

MELINDA
Like I care.

REGGIE
Please don't make it a murder mystery.

MELINDA
Oh, but I love a good mystery.

REGGIE
That's what I was afraid of.

DONNA
Can we pick it then?

CAPTAIN
You? Oh, and I suppose you'll need a computer to search for one?

DONNA
Well, now that you mention it...

CAPTAIN
Forget it. Check out the prison library. I'm sure they have Shakespeare or something.

MELINDA
This crew doing Shakespeare? This might be fun after all.

(CAPTAIN looks around)

CAPTAIN
Where's Gus? Gus!

(Appears from behind a curtain. His clothes are a little messed up. CAPTAIN is more focused on MELINDA so he doesn't really notice)

GUS
Right here, sir. Just checking out the perimeter. Making sure it's secure.

CAPTAIN
Get this place cleaned up, okay? Shall we, Ms. Street?

(CAPTAIN leads MELINDA out)

REGGIE
So where were you Gus? And where's Macy?

GUS
I don't know what you mean?

(MACY enters with a mirror and straightens her hair)

REGGIE
Oh, there she is. I wonder where you two were?

GUS
We two? No. Not two. Not us.

REGGIE
You're a bad liar, Gus. You're just lucky that Ms. Street had the captain's eye.

MACY
So we cleaning this place or not?

DONNA
In a minute. We need to have a little talk, girls.

GUS
What about?

DONNA
Hair, nails, makeup...

(REGGIE gives GUS a mean look)

REGGIE
PMS...

GUS
Guess I'll do another perimeter check.

MACY
I'll help...

(MACY follows GUS out)

DONNA
That will keep Gus busy.

REGGIE
So what's the plan? I can tell you got something cooking.

DONNA
I think this play may provide us with a little opportunity.

REGGIE
Opportunity for what?

(DONNA looks to make sure GUS isn't close by)

DONNA
To escape.

REGGIE
What?!

DONNA
Keep your voice down.

REGGIE
Why do you want to escape? You're not a red-shirt.

DONNA
But I'm going to be here a long time. The company I hacked and the government are making sure of that. They want to make an example of me. A warning to all hackers was what they said at my trial. They were at my last parole hearing and they were pushing to throw way the key.

REGGIE
Then why don't you just run off now while Goofy's on the job?

DONNA
In these clothes, I don't think so. They'd track me down in no time.

REGGIE
So you're thinking, you'll pick a play that gets you in street clothes.

DONNA
Exactly.

REGGIE
That rules out Shakespeare then. Imagine trying to escape in one of them outfits. You'd look like Cinderella running from the ball.

DONNA
And with Ms. Street involved, we'll have a big crowd. Plus everyone will be focused on her. I'll just blend in and slip away.

REGGIE
So why you telling us about this?

DONNA
Thought maybe you'd like to join me.

REGGIE
Now why would I want to go and give up all this? Three meals a day, cable tv, pizza parties on Fridays... I've got it made.

DONNA
And how did your last parole hearing go?

REGGIE
Not good.

DONNA
How come?

REGGIE
Well, I kind of made the warden mad and who knows how long that will keep me here.

DONNA
What'd you do?

REGGIE
Our good warden was trying to get me to use my skills to line his pocketbook.

DONNA
You're kidding?

REGGIE
Nope. The guy was needing some extra cash and he knew I could get it for him.

DONNA
You're that good?

REGGIE
I'm that good. Better than you, hacker girl, because I'm assuming he hasn't asked for your assistance?

DONNA
Nope. So if you're so good at passing fake checks then how'd you get caught?

REGGIE
My momma turned me in.

DONNA
Ouch.

REGGIE
She got all religious and ethical on me. Tried to convince I was a modern day Robin Hood...

DONNA
Taking from the rich and giving to the poor huh?

REGGIE
Well, I was about as poor as they come. I think I was a worthy cause.

DONNA
I totally agree. I'm my favorite cause.

REGGIE
What about Macy? You think she'll do it.

DONNA
She's up for parole and I don't think she wants to stray far from Gus... but I think she'll help. She may prove to be a good distraction for our personal guard.

REGGIE
What about Melinda? She could be the spoiler of this little plan of yours.

DONNA
No, she's central to making this work.

REGGIE
As long as she doesn't catch on.

              DONNA
         So what do you say?

              12006
              I'm in.

(Big smile from DONNA and they look at REGGIE)

              REGGIE
         Okay, okay. I'm in too.

              DONNA
    I'll get the play. You two start packing.

              REGGIE
You better not mess this up or 12006 is gonna be pretty
                upset.

              DONNA
      And I don't want to upset 12006.

    (REGGIE looks around and speaks up)

              REGGIE
     So how's that perimeter looking, Gus?

         (MACY giggles off stage)

              DONNA
      Pretty good by the sounds of it.

            MACY (off)
You naughty, naughty prison. I've got some work detail for
             you. Bend over.

              REGGIE
         I didn't need to hear that.

   (Lights fade to black as they clean again)

ACT II

(The theatre is looking in better condition. The garbage is gone and stage now has nice shine to it. DONNA, REGGIE, 12006 enter looking pleased. MACY follows GUS in and CAPTAIN escorts MELINDA. They work on putting up the set during the scene when they aren't practicing the play)

DONNA
The stage is so shiny you can see your reflection. Just like you wanted Captain.

CAPTAIN
Will this work, Ms. Street?

MELINDA
We're really going through with this?

MACY
Donna found a great play.

MELINDA
Oh, joy. What great play are we going to defile?

REGGIE
I thought you'd be perfect for the Best Little Whore House in Texas but Donna found something else.

MELINDA
Oh, you're so funny.

(DONNA hands out copies of the script)

DONNA
Here's the script. It's not anything known but it fits us nicely.

MELINDA
Why? Is it about a bunch of no talent criminals? REGGIE
Oh, I'm so hurt.

DONNA
It is about an actress who gets her chance to be famous.

MELINDA
(Sounding bored)
I suppose I'll be playing the actress.

DONNA
Actually no.

MELINDA
(Slightly offended)
I won't?

DONNA
I thought Reggie should play the main character.

MELINDA
Her? You think she can carry the play. This will be amusing.

DONNA
But it has an awesome part for you. You'd play the fortune teller, Madame Mooch. It's a great part. The best one in the show really.

MELINDA
I'll take a look.

CAPTAIN
You can have whatever part you want, Ms. Street. After all, this is all about you.

MELINDA
The less time on stage the better. You seem to assume that I'm anxious to be doing this.

DONNA
Macy, you'll be playing Reggie's best friend Heather. She's kind of the comic relief.

MACY
Cool.

MELINDA
Good choice.

MACY
Really?

MELINDA
Yes, I laugh just looking at you.

MACY
Thanks.

MELINDA
That wasn't a compliment.

DONNA
I'll be the talent agent who discovers the actress. And 12006. You'll be the psycho killer who storms onto the set.

MELINDA
Type casting huh?

(12006 gives MELINDA a killer look but she winks back)

CAPTAIN
You're giving her lines? Can she even speak?

DONNA
Yes, she can speak.

MELINDA
And how do get her to do that? Scooby snacks?

DONNA
She'll be fine.

(GUS has been looking at script)

GUS
Psycho killer? Hey, she can't have a gun or anything.

DONNA
Don't worry. We won't use a real gun. And Gus, we want you to be the cop that saves the day.

MACY
Gus will be in it too?

GUS
You mean like I'll kind of be the hero?

MACY
How exciting. I've always seen you as the hero type.

MELINDA
Fine, I've got the script. Can I go now?

REGGIE
Uh, we need to practice...

MELINDA
You need to practice. I need my yoga session.

CAPTAIN
Is it time for your yoga already?

MELINDA
Meditation first. Then yoga. Memorize the schedule, Captain.

(MELINDA exits and CAPTAIN follows)

CAPTAIN
(Mockingly)
"Memorize the schedule, Captain."

(CAPTAIN exits)

DONNA
I see the captain's patience is wearing thin.

GUS
He's been made her personal guard and he isn't liking it much. Well at first he did but she's treating him like an errand boy so it's getting old fast.

REGGIE
So how'd the captain get stuck with her?

GUS
He asked for the assignment but now he's sorry.

REGGIE
So how we going to practice this thing without her?

DONNA
That's why I didn't make her the main character. Her part isn't that big. But it's a good one that should fit her.

MACY
Why? Is she playing an ice queen with a stick up her butt?

REGGIE
Whoa... is this the same girl who was falling all over herself to talk to Melinda before?

MACY
I don't understand why she doesn't like me. What have I done to her. I mean I practically worship her and all she does is throw insults at me and trashes my presents.

REGGIE
Presents? What presents?

MACY
Well, I've written her a letter almost every day since she's been here and she hasn't written back. In fact she trashes my letters.

REGGIE
And how do you know that?

MACY
I go through her trash.

REGGIE
I had to ask.

MACY
And I made her these little pictures with me and her doing things together like going to movie premieres and going to the beach...

REGGIE
How do you do that?

MACY
I cut pictures out of magazines of her and take photos of me and put them together. I sometimes put my head on pictures of Pamela Anderson when I can find them because we have real similar figures.

(MACY winks at GUS who blushes)

REGGIE
And she doesn't like the pictures either huh?

MACY
No, she ripped up the last one right in front of me. I swear I'm going to resign as the president of her fan club.

REGGIE
Macy, you know what they call people like you?

MACY
What?

REGGIE
They call you stalkers. You're like one of them weirdoes that follow celebrities around and search for hairs that they leave on restaurant chairs and make wigs out of them.

MACY
I do not make wigs. She doesn't shed nearly enough for that.

REGGIE
You know your girl here was a little too obsessed?

MACY
I have another obsession that Gussie doesn't mind.

(GUS tries not to smile but can't help it)

DONNA
So everyone okay with their parts?

REGGIE
No offense 12006, but you okay with doing a part in a play?

(12006 shrugs)

DONNA
She'll be fine.

GUS
So am I really the hero?

DONNA
You do come save everyone in the end.

GUS
How many lines I got? I haven't found any yet.

DONNA
Well, not too many, but your role is pivotal to the production.

MACY
Pivotal, Gussie. That sounds neat.

REGGIE
(Aside to DONNA)
She even know what pivotal means?

(DONNA shrugs)

GUS
I guess that means I'll have to stay assigned as your guard throughout the production then.

DONNA
That's what I'm hoping.

(DONNA and REGGIE smile knowingly)

MACY
Oh, Gussie. This will be so fun.

GUS
So what am I?

REGGIE
A goober.

GUS
In the play?

DONNA
You're the cop that comes and stops the psycho gunman.

REGGIE
Think you can take, 12006?

(12006 has come up behind GUS who turns and jumps)

GUS
Uh...

MACY
Don't worry, Gussie. We're just playacting.

REGGIE
That's what you think.

GUS
Maybe we should pick a different play. This one might be too dangerous.

MACY
It'll be fine, Gussie. It's all pretend.

REGGIE
Hey, why don't you pretend like you're a delivery guy and get us some pizza? I'm starving.

GUS
Pizza? Who said you got pizza?

REGGIE
The warden.

(GUS looks nervous)

GUS
He did?

REGGIE
Sure did. And do you want to disobey the warden?

GUS
No. But why would he say you get pizza?

REGGIE
Because of Melinda Street. Only the best for her.

GUS
But she isn't here.

REGGIE
That's her problem isn't it.

MACY
Pizza does sound good, Gussie.

GUS
I guess I can call and check.

REGGIE
You calling me a liar?

GUS
Yes. Macy? What do you know about this?

(MACY does a cute, pouty routine)

MACY
Not much really. But I sure would like some pizza though. I'm so hungry.

GUS
I guess pizza wouldn't hurt then. I'll go call it in. I'll be right back.

MACY
Thanks, Gussie. You're my hero.

(GUS blushes and exits)

REGGIE
Girl, I love it when you work your magic.

MACY
Mamma always said if you can't get a man to do what you want then he ain't worth doing.

REGGIE
That's some twisted Forest Gump wisdom, but I like it.

MACY
So, Donna? I got rid of Gus like you asked. What's up?

DONNA
I picked this play because it has the perfect opportunity to escape. There's this whole bit with a false wall. And that false wall will be our ticket out.

REGGIE
But at what point in the play? You're on stage the whole time.

DONNA
We do it at the curtain call. We do our bows and then Melinda does her bows last. They'll be so into her they won't even notice we're gone.

MACY
But what about Gus? Won't he be back there with us?

DONNA
That's your job. Can you make sure Gus is distracted?

MACY
Oh, yeah.

REGGIE
What if Gus be isn't the only guard?

DONNA
I'm working on that part still.

REGGIE
Oh, great. So this isn't a sure thing?

DONNA
Trust me. I'll work out.

REGGIE
Nail it down or I'm not bothering.

DONNA
Look, they always leave Gus to watch us. Why should that change?

REGGIE
I'll bet they have extra security because of Melinda. What are we going to do about those extra guards if they do?

MACY
You could drop one of those lights up there on her. Those guards would sure scramble then.

DONNA
We'll call that plan B.

REGGIE
Girl, you do have a mean side after all.

MACY
You sure we can't drop that on her just for fun?

DONNA
If you want to become a red shirt.

MACY
No, red's not my color.

DONNA
Plus you're almost out of here. Why blow it?

REGGIE
So you're not escaping with us, Macy?

MACY
What's the point? My time is almost up and if I ran Gussie and I couldn't...

REGGIE
Couldn't what? Expand your beanie baby collection?

DONNA
Don't tell me you guys are gonna do it?

MACY
Maybe... but Gussie made me promise not to tell.

REGGIE
Wow, that's great. Gus get the ring or you gonna shoplift your own?

MACY
Ha, ha. Very funny.

(MACY pouts)

DONNA
What's wrong?

MACY
I just realized that I can't even shop for my own ring.
Parole violation.

REGGIE
And I can imagine what Gus will get.

DONNA
You could shop online.

MACY Online, catalogs... that's like pure torture... I have to touch them. See them sparkle.

REGGIE
Oh, no. Her eyes are glazing over.

MACY
I saw this wedding dress once that sparkled like diamonds. It was an outdoor wedding and the sun lit her up... Oh, it was the most beautiful thing I've ever seen.

REGGIE
We're losing her.

MACY
And they can play my favorite song at wedding as I walking like a giant diamond to Gus...

DONNA
She's gone.
(MACY is lost in some fantasy and starts singing)

MACY
"Diamonds are a girls... best... friend..."

REGGIE
Oh, good. Here comes Gus now.

(MACY snaps out of it)

MACY
Please don't tell him I told you.

(REGGIE hums the wedding march as GUS enters)

REGGIE
Dum, dum, da, dum. Dum, da, dum, dum.

MACY
Shush...

GUS
Sorry, girls. No pizza.

REGGIE
And why not?

GUS
Captain said no. Melinda's coming back and she's on a diet.

REGGIE
Diet? Figures. So we get nothing.

GUS
Like celery sticks?

REGGIE
Oh, yes. That's my favorite wedding food.

GUS
Huh?

MACY
Shush up.

DONNA
So Melinda's coming back now?

GUS
Captain said she punched her yoga instructor so she's got some extra time now.

(MELINDA enters with CAPTAIN)

REGGIE
What did her yoga instructor do?

MELINDA
He got too nosey.

REGGIE
Oh, I'm so scared.

CAPTAIN
Gus, I've got an errand to run. Think you can handle Ms. Street for a bit?

GUS
No problem, Captain. I can keep things under control.

CAPTAIN
I want to see some drama therapy going on when I get back too.

DONNA
Got it covered, Captain. Let's start from the top. Everyone got your scripts.

(CAPTAIN exits. MELINDA goes over to GUS and acts sexy)

MELINDA
Mind if I step out for a bit, Gus?

GUS
Uh, no... I mean you can't. It's not allowed.

MELINDA
Just for a second. I promise I'll be right back.

MACY
Get away from him.

MELINDA
Oh, what's the mater? Am I getting a little too close.

(MELINDA leans on GUS and blows in his ear. MACY grabs her)

MACY
Hands off.

MELINDA
Don't touch me.

(MELINDA pulls free of MACY)

MACY
Touch you... like this.

(MACY pokes MELINDA. GUS jumps between them)

GUS
Back off, Ms. Street or you'll spend the rest of your drama therapy time in handcuffs.

MELINDA
Oh, I'm so scared. Little police man's gonna handcuff me. Or is that a game you like to play with the girls?

MACY
I'm going to kill her.

GUS
Macy, please. Don't.

MELINDA
Look, ladies. If you want to act with me you've got to follow a few simple rules.

REGGIE
This will be good.

MELINDA
When I'm on stage, you all back up and give me room.

(REGGIE says following under her breath)

REGGIE
With hips like that, I can see why.

MELINDA
What did you say?

REGGIE
I said with chips and dip I want to buy.

MELINDA
What's that supposed to mean?

REGGIE
Nothing, nothing. On with the reglas...

MELINDA
The key is to stay upstage of me at all times. (Points upstage) That's upstage. And I will be downstage. (She wakes downstage regally)

MACY
What if we're talking to you? You want us to do it from back here?

MELINDA
Exactly.

MACY
Won't that look funny?

MELINDA
Who is the actor here? Me. So let me handle this.

(MACY pleads with DONNA)

MACY
Donna... are we really doing it this way?

DONNA
Don't worry about it, Macy.

MELINDA
Good attitude, Dina.

DONNA
Donna.

MELINDA
Whatever. The key, girls, is to not steal my light. You'll have your time to play act while I'm off stage.

MACY
But... Donna.

MELINDA
"But... Donna." Nothing. That's the way it's going to be.

DONNA
It'll be fine. Let's do the scene where Jo, the gunman, enters.

12006
Where's my gun?

(DONNA pulls some stuff from a prop box. She finds a rubber chicken and give it to 12006 who gives her a dirty look)

DONNA
It'll have to do for now. You know how hard it is to find anything that is anywhere close to a gun.

12006
I'll find one.

(12006 goes upstage with rubber chicken)

REGGIE
I can always make one in pottery class.

MACY
One of the inmates said you can make a gun out of part from our cell toilets.

REGGIE
Okay, you get right on that, McGyver.

DONNA
Let's get in our places. Page 23.

(MACY goes downstage and MELINDA glares at her)

MACY
What? You're not even on stage yet.

MELINDA
Fine.

(MELINDA steps off stage and passes REGGIE)

REGGIE
Whoa... nearly got knocked over.

MELINDA
I wasn't even close to you.

REGGIE
But I'm imagining that you have this big diva bubble around you. It's so big.

MELINDA
Whatever.

(REGGIE goes to 12006)

REGGIE
They're her "virtual hips." Huge.

(DONNA goes off to side with 12006. MELINDA is off the other side and MACY and REGGIE are waiting upstage)

DONNA
Okay, Jo. You enter through the door really angry and then say your line...

(12006 doesn't respond. DONNA goes to her)

DONNA (CONT.)
12006. You're Jo and here's your first line. Ready?
(12006 looks at the script and squints)
Everything okay?

12006
(Quietly)
Can't read.

DONNA
Oh, man. I'm sorry.

12006
I don't need your pity.

DONNA
Well, maybe we can adapt this a bit. I'll talk you through it.

(12006 nods)

MELINDA
Let's get going people.

DONNA
Okay, so 12006. You rush in and wave your chicken... I mean gun... and say "Where's Madame Mooch?"

(12006 rushes in with chicken)

12006
Where's Mooch?

DONNA
Close enough.

REGGIE/BRENDA
She's in her secret room laughing at us no doubt.
(Tries to go as does MACY)
Can we get by please?

DONNA
Don't let them by.

(12006 tackles REGGIE and MACY)

REGGIE
Hey!

DONNA
No, no, no. Just stand in their way.

REGGIE
I didn't think plays were so dangerous.

MELINDA
Sometimes they're deadly.

(REGGIE rolls her eyes)

DONNA
Okay, Jo. Your next line is "I want to see Mooch now!"

12006
Where's Mooch?

DONNA
That'll work.

REGGIE/BRENDA
All you have to do is wave a few dollars around. She'll appear.
(Falls out of character)
Ha, this is like type casting huh?

MELINDA
Shut up.

DONNA
Then you say "Maybe if I wave this instead..."

                    12006
               (Holds up gun)
              Where's Mooch?

                    DONNA
            Good improvising. I like it.

                 MACY/HEATHER
                She's got a gun!

                REGGIE/BRENDA
        Hey, now lady. We don't want any trouble.

                    DONNA
Now you say, "Well, that's what you're going to get unless
                  I see Mooch."
        (12006 gives her an annoyed look)
    Or you could just say "Where's Mooch?" again.

                    12006
              Where's Mooch?

                    DONNA
                  Very nice.

                REGGIE/BRENDA
I don't know what your problem with her is, but it has
         nothing to do with us. So if we could just go…

                    DONNA
How about we skip all this silly dialog by Jo and you can
          just force them into some chairs.

(12006 pushes REGGIE into a chair and MACY quickly goes
                    to hers)

                    REGGIE
Warn us will you, Donna? This is worse than football.

DONNA
Now for your line, Reggie.

REGGIE/BRENDA
You know what? No crime has been committed. As far as I can tell, you have a permit for that gun. No crime. No problem. Let's go, Heather.

(They start to get up and 12006 pushes REGGIE down)

DONNA
Good improvising.

REGGIE
Yeah, great.

DONNA
And let's have Mooch come out now.

(MELINDA comes out in a persona of a fortuneteller)

MELINDA/MOOCH
Hello, Jo. What do you want?

DONNA
And Jo goes, blah, blah, blah and Madama Mooch says...

MELINDA/MOOCH
I'll bet that gun isn't even loaded.

DONNA
Okay, Jo, now pretend to shoot the gun.

(12006 pretends to shoot chicken at MELINDA/MOOCH MELINDA/MOOCH faints while MACY/HEATHER screams)

MELINDA
(back to self)
That was the most pitiful scream I've heard yet.

MACY
Here, let me try again...

MELINDA
Forget it. Just let me finish my fainting before you do it. It'll distract from my moment.

MACY
That's not what the script says. It says I scream while you faint.

MELINDA
Well, if you could handle it as written I'd be all for it, but I think we need to adapt things a bit for our less experienced actresses.

MACY
I'm so sick of you talking down to us. You're nothing but a big... stuck up... meanie.

MELINDA
Oh, that was harsh. Careful you might hurt my feelings.

(REGGIE goes up behind MELINDA)

REGGIE
You're not as big and bad as you pretend to be. Bet you killed all those people by accident. You're big on talk but little on the walk.

(MELINDA spins and grabs REGGIE's arm and twists and REGGIE goes down and MELINDA ends up with a knee in REGGIE's back and REGGIE is face down on the floor)

MELINDA
How's that?

REGGIE
Pretty good.

GUS
Let her up.

MELINDA
Oh, but I was just starting to have some fun.

GUS
I'm putting you in cuffs.

MELINDA
I'd like to see you try.

GUS
I've been trained to handle prisoners like you.

MELINDA
I once took out Arnold Swartzenagger so I'm not scared.

(GUS and MELINDA face off and GUS looks scared. GUS goes for the take-down and MELINDA grabs him and pins him)

MELINDA (CONT.)
What you going to do now, copper?

(MACY grabs MELINDA by the hair and pulls her off GUS. MELINDA tries to swing at MACY but she dodges and then puts her in a choke hold and slowly chokes the air out of her)

REGGIE
This is better than wrestling.

MACY
Say you're sorry.

(MELINDA shakes her head no and then MACY squeezes more and MELINDA crumples to her knees. MELINDA gasps)

DONNA
I think she's trying to say something, Macy.

MACY
Say it...

MELINDA
Sorry.

(MACY releases her and REGGIE feels MACY's arms)

REGGIE
Yow, girl. You work out?

MACY
I grew up with seven brothers. I can hold my own.

(MACY goes to GUS)

GUS
Macy, you didn't need to do that.

MACY
I don't mind, Gussie.

GUS
I guess I better cuff her now.

(GUS is still scared)

MACY
No, she woke be any trouble now. Will you?
(MELINDA gives her a dirty look and MACY steps toward her)
Will you?

MELINDA
No.

REGGIE
Maybe we should just do that on stage. That was entertainment.

(CAPTAIN enters)

CAPTAIN
Everything okay in here?

(They all look at MELINDA unsure what she'll say)

MELINDA
Everything's fine.

CAPTAIN
Let's get back to the prison. It's almost dinner. Chef's surprise tonight.

REGGIE
Gotta love that Chef's surprise. The surprise for me is if I can keep it down.

(CAPTAIN exits with REGGIE and 12006. GUS escorts MACY. MELINDA stops DONNA)

MELINDA
I know what you're planning.

(DONNA plays dumb)

DONNA
I don't know you mean.

(DONNA starts to go but MELINDA stops her)

MELINDA
I want you to help me escape too.

(DONNA is surprised and drops her dumb act)

DONNA
That will be impossible. You're the whole reason this was going to work.

MELINDA
Guess I'll just tell the captain now about your plans.

DONNA
You would, would you?

MELINDA
Without a doubt.

DONNA
Fine, you're in.

MELINDA
I think I'm starting to like this play.

(MELINDA exits)

DONNA
How am I going to pull this off now?

(Lights fade to black)

ACT III

(Set is complete. The set is of Madame Mooch's parlor. Part of the back wall has beads across it with false wall the can be moved and replaced. As the audience comes in from intermission, MACY, DONNA, REGGIE, GUS and 12006 are putting finishing touches on the set with the CAPTAIN watching. MELINDA is doing her nails)

MACY
They're here!

DONNA
Let's get back stage.

(MELINDA to DONNA as she exits)

MELINDA
Don't blow it.

REGGIE
Is that something like break a leg?

DONNA
I think she will break my leg if I'm not careful.

CAPTAIN
I'll be out here, ladies and Gus will be watching back stage.

MACY
You mean Gus will be back there watching us change costumes?

REGGIE
He can turn his back.

MACY
No peeking.

CAPTAIN
We have guards at every entrance to this place. Don't think about trying anything.

DONNA
No worries, Captain.
(CAPTAIN goes and sits in audience)

REGGIE
Ready?

DONNA
Ready.

(All exit and intro music plays and lights go to black a moment. Lights come up a moment later with REGGIE on stage as BRENDA)

REGGIE/BRENDA
This is so stupid... can we go now? It's Saturday night and there's other places I'd rather be...

MACY/HEATHER
(Rushes in from being beaded curtain) You'll never guess who she said I was in one of my past lives.

REGGIE/BRENDA
Let's see. Cleopatra?

MACY/HEATHER
How did you know?

REGGIE/BRENDA
Psychic's always say women were Cleopatra... For some reason, everyone wants to be her. Personally, I'd rather have been someone longer lived. What a way to go. Snake bite to the breast. Ouch.

MACY/HEATHER
You don't think it's true?

REGGIE/BRENDA
Heather, these people aren't for real. Don't you read the disclaimers?
(Holds up brochure)
For entertainment purposes only.

MACY/HEATHER
She seems so real... so convincing...

MELINDA/MOOCH
(Enters from beaded curtained area)
Oh, sorry. I didn't know anyone was still here?

REGGIE/BRENDA
I can see she's real psychic.

(MELINDA/MOOCH points to a table with a crystal ball on top and two chairs)

MELINDA/MOOCH
Does you friend want a reading?

MACY/HEATHER
Yes!

REGGIE/BRENDA
No!

MACY/HEATHER
Come on, Brenda. I'll pay for it.

REGGIE/BRENDA
Don't waste your money.

MACY/HEATHER
It's just for fun. You said it yourself: for entertainment purposes only. What do you have to fear?

REGGIE/BRENDA
Fear itself?

MELINDA/MOOCH
Come, come. I won't bite.

REGGIE/BRENDA
Yeah, but I might.

MACY/HEATHER
There, I paid for it.

(Gives MOOCH money)

MELINDA/MOOCH
(Holds bill up to light)
I feel my power returning to me.

REGGIE/BRENDA
The power of the U.S. Mint.

MACY/HEATHER
Go on.

REGGIE/BRENDA
(Goes UC)
Fine, let's get this over with.

MELINDA/MOOCH
The spirits come to me.

MACY/HEATHER
You sure you want me to watch. It gets kind of private.
(Sits in a nearby waiting room chair)

REGGIE/BRENDA
I want witnesses in case she goes for my purse.
(Sits in chair by crystal ball)

MELINDA/MOOCH
(Sits in other chair)
So what do you want to know?

REGGIE/BRENDA
The quickest way out of here.

MACY/HEATHER
Don't be difficult, Brenda. Try to have fun with it.

REGGIE/BRENDA
Fine. What are this week's winning lottery numbers?

MELINDA/MOOCH
3-5-9-20-25-49 and the Powerball is...
(Draws card from Taro deck)
7.

REGGIE/BRENDA
Pretty specific.

MACY/HEATHER
(Writes the numbers down)
Why didn't I think to ask that?

REGGIE/BRENDA
What else do you see in the cards?

MELINDA/MOOCH
(Draws more cards)
I see your past and your future.

REGGIE/BRENDA
Let me guess. I was Cleopatra too. How is it possible for so many people to be Cleopatra? I know... maybe she had a split personality.

MELINDA/MOOCH
I'm afraid in your past you were nobody famous.

REGGIE/BRENDA
(Surprisingly disappointed)
Nobody? Ever?

MELINDA/MOOCH
Never ever.

REGGIE/BRENDA
What about my future?

MELINDA/MOOCH
You will be famous one day.

REGGIE/BRENDA
Now or in a future life.

MELINDA/MOOCH
Would you like to be famous in this life?

REGGIE/BRENDA
What do you mean?

MELINDA/MOOCH
In everyone's life cycles, they are allowed one time to be famous.

REGGIE/BRENDA
Only once huh?
(Amused. Smiles at HEATHER)

MELINDA/MOOCH
Do you wish it to be this one?

REGGIE/BRENDA
(Laughs)
Sure, why not?

MELINDA/MOOCH
(Her voice booms)
Then so be it!
(A big boom, like thunder is heard. The lights flicker and go out. When the lights come on again MOOCH is gone)

REGGIE/BRENDA
That was weird.

MACY/HEATHER
(Rushes to BRENDA and looks around table)
Where'd she go?

REGGIE/BRENDA
Behind the beads no doubt.

MACY/HEATHER
(Checks behind beads)
It's solid wall behind here now!

REGGIE/BRENDA
Then through a trap door. It doesn't matter. Let's go.

MACY/HEATHER
(They head for front door)
You have to admit. That was pretty spooky.

REGGIE/BRENDA
And completely fake.
(Mimics MOOCH)
"You can only be famous once in your life cycles."
(Laughs)
What a fraud. She's not even a good fake psychic.

12006/JO
(Enters through front door looking around)
Where's Mooch?

REGGIE/BRENDA
She vanished.

(12006 looks confused. She sees audience, gets nervous and then stares at them like a deer in a headlight)

MACY/HEATHER
Oh, hey, there total stranger. Aren't surprised to see Brenda here?

(12006 still stares blankly at audience)

DONNA
(off)
Yes, hey, aren't you that famous actress?

REGGIE/BRENDA
Who? Me?

DONNA
(off)
Yeah, the actress in the play downtown. What's it called? A Brush with Destiny. That's it.

MACY/HEATHER
Did you see her?

DONNA
(off)
Yeah, you were incredible.

(MACY takes 12006's arm and pats REGGIE on the shoulder. 12006 is still staring at audience)

REGGIE/BRENDA
Thanks.

DONNA
(off)
Did you see the review in today's paper?

(DONNA throws in paper from off stage and MACY sticks it in 12006's hand)

MACY/HEATHER
You got a review?
(Takes paper and looks)

REGGIE/BRENDA
That local theatre reviewer is an idiot. He wouldn't know a play if a stage fell on him.

MACY/HEATHER
Oh, my gosh. This review is really good.

REGGIE/BRENDA
You're kidding. He never likes anything.

MACY/HEATHER
(Reads)
Brenda Star lives up to her name. Her radiant talent brightens this otherwise ordinary play.

REGGIE/BRENDA
Let me see that.
(Takes paper)
This is so great! My agent will go nuts.

(They look at 12006 who has a line)

MACY/HEATHER
I guess you better run and come back to see if Mooch is here later.
(MACY/HEATHER guides 12006/JO off stage)
We better go get a copy of the paper so you can show your agent.

REGGIE/BRENDA
Wait a minute. This smells like a set up.

MACY/HEATHER
What do you mean?

REGGIE/BRENDA
Wasn't that awfully good timing? She says I'm going to be famous and then this person comes in here and acts like I'm some new star.

MACY/HEATHER
But how could she fake that newspaper review?

REGGIE/BRENDA
(Scowls)
Good point.

MACY/HEATHER
So do you think there might be something to this psychic thing?

REGGIE/BRENDA
It's a coincidence. That's all.
(Cell phone rings)
Hello? Hi, Gina.
(To MACY/HEATHER)
It's my agent.

MACY/HEATHER
I'll bet she saw the review.

REGGIE/BRENDA
Yeah, I read it.
(Pause)
Very good.
(Shocked)
What?
(Pause)
No way.

MACY/HEATHER
What is it? What?

REGGIE/BRENDA
(Waves away MACY/HEATHER)
Shhhh.
(To phone)
Sorry, my friend is talking to me.
(Pause)
Yes, let's do it.
(Looks around)
I hate to admit this, but I'm at some psychic reading place.
(Picks up brochure)
Madame Mooch…
(Pause)
You know her.
(To MACY/HEATHER)
My agent's been here.
(Pause)
Sure I'll wait for her here.
(Hangs up phone)
You won't believe this.

MACY/HEATHER
Probably not, but tell me anyway.

REGGIE/BRENDA
Somebody is filming a movie in town and they saw my show last night. They want me to be in their movie.

MACY/HEATHER
You're kidding?

REGGIE/BRENDA
Gina said there are some big stars in it too. One of them had a scheduling conflict and can't come. Gina's sending the casting director over to see me now. They need somebody immediately and want me to do it.

MACY/HEATHER
You'll be famous!

REGGIE/BRENDA
(Stops)
This can't be happening. Where is that Madame Money?

MACY/HEATHER
Mooch.

REGGIE/BRENDA
Whatever. Come out, Madame! I want a word with you.

MACY/HEATHER
Why are you upset? This is wonderful.

REGGIE/BRENDA
I know how these stories go. Remember that story the Monkey's Paw? At first, everything is great. You get everything you wish for, then the bottom drops out.

MACY/HEATHER
You are such a wet blanket. Can't you have a little fun?

REGGIE/BRENDA
Fun is for people who are too stupid to prepare for the impending disaster.

MACY/HEATHER
I give up. Fine, don't enjoy your instant success. I'm going home.

REGGIE/BRENDA
Don't be mad, Heather. I'm sorry. I have to admit there might be something beyond my comprehension going on here.

MACY/HEATHER
See! Isn't this stuff amazing?

REGGIE/BRENDA
Or extremely well contrived.
(Calls out)
Madame Mooch. I need a word with you.

MACY/HEATHER
I wonder why she isn't reappearing.

REGGIE/BRENDA
(Pulls out money)
I'm not speaking her language.
(Waves bill)
I have something green for you.

MELINDA/MOOCH
(Enters)
I sense that you require my services.

REGGIE/BRENDA
(Smiles at HEATHER, then looks at MOOCH)
I need some information.

MELINDA/MOOCH
Information is my middle name, though my abilities have been weakened by all the recent activity.

REGGIE/BRENDA
(Hands her a bill)
There. Feeling better?

MELINDA/MOOCH
A bit better, yes.

REGGIE/BRENDA
Good.

MELINDA/MOOCH
I sense your friend here wants to go.

REGGIE/BRENDA
Do you?

MACY/HEATHER
(Looks at watch)
Oh, my gosh. I have reservations for five minutes ago.
(Waves good-bye)
Thank you, Madame Mooch. Bye Brenda.

(HEATHER exits)

REGGIE/BRENDA
That was my money. How come she got a reading?

MELINDA/MOOCH
She paid for you. You paid for her.

REGGIE/BRENDA
Now for my question...

MELINDA/MOOCH
My power is fading.

REGGIE/BRENDA
(Hands her another bill)
Feel better?

MELINDA/MOOCH
(Stuffs bill in shirt)
Ask your question.

REGGIE/BRENDA
How can Madame Mooch cook up such an elaborate scam?

MELINDA/MOOCH
Madame Mooch didn't scam you. You want to be famous, so you will be famous.

REGGIE/BRENDA
What if I've changed my mind?

MELINDA/MOOCH
It is your destiny now. Don't fight it. Fighting it will only bring doom upon you.

REGGIE/BRENDA
Doom. That's certainly what I'm expecting from all this. Every silver lining has a cloud.

MELINDA/MOOCH
I predict that your bad fortune is over.

REGGIE/BRENDA
I hope you're right.

MELINDA/MOOCH
Unless...

REGGIE/BRENDA
There's always an unless... Okay, give me the bad news.

MELINDA/MOOCH
I must consult the cards. (Goes to her table)

REGGIE/BRENDA
That's probably going to cost me.
(Goes to table and sits opposite MOOCH)

MELINDA/MOOCH
(Lays out some cards)
The meaning of these cards escape me...
(REGGIE/BRENDA sighs and gives her more money)
Ah, yes. I see now. Beware the one armed bandit.

REGGIE/BRENDA
You mean slot machines? That's easy. I hate gambling. Ever since that time my boyfriend got kidnapped by a trucker at Sky City Casino, I've refused to go back to one.

MELINDA/MOOCH
(Rises)
Beware. Beware the one armed bandit.

REGGIE/BRENDA
Yeah, yeah. You said that already.
(MELINDA/MOOCH starts to go)
Wait. I have more questions.

MELINDA/MOOCH
No time. You have a visitor.

(Exits as BONNIE enters front door)

REGGIE/BRENDA
How did she know that?

DONNA/BONNIE
Brenda Star! It's wonderful to see you.
(They do a fake kiss on the cheek)
How does it feel to make the lead story of Theatre Scene Magazine?

REGGIE/BRENDA
I did?

DONNA/BONNIE
I guess the issue did just come out. Here it is.
(Hands her a magazine)
Great picture of you.

REGGIE/BRENDA
Wow, this is incredible.

DONNA/BONNIE
I should introduce myself. I'm Bonnie Bandito.

(Reaches out her hand to shake. BONNIE lifts her left arm to shake. BONNIE's right arm is in a sling)

REGGIE/BRENDA
Bandito? Oh...
(Looks where MOOCH went)
Uh... hi...

DONNA/BONNIE
Something wrong?

REGGIE/BRENDA
Sorry, this has all been very sudden. I'm pretty new to all this.

DONNA/BONNIE
But you're a natural. You appear to have years of experience. If it's okay, I'd like to interview you a bit first.

REGGIE/BRENDA
Yes, I have a few questions also.

(They sit)

DONNA/BONNIE
Would you like to go first or shall I?

REGGIE/BRENDA
I'll go first. The main question on my mind is why would a big studio want a little small time nobody like me?

DONNA/BONNIE
You have the look...

REGGIE/BRENDA
(Skeptically)
The look?

(DONNA/BONNIE hands her a promo packet on the movie)

DONNA/BONNIE
You have that natural spark that will light up the screen...
La Chizpa as they say. And to be honest, you are very
attractive and our director liked you... a lot. He's known for
taking many unknown actresses and making them big
stars.

REGGIE/BRENDA
(Looks in packet)
This director is also known for wanting a whole lot more
from his actresses than is in the contract.

DONNA/BONNIE
He's very influential... he could take you far.

REGGIE/BRENDA
(Hands back the packet to BONNIE)
I'd rather he didn't take me anywhere.

DONNA/BONNIE
What? You're not going to do it?

REGGIE/BRENDA
How big of a part is this?

DONNA/BONNIE
That depends on you.

REGGIE/BRENDA
What does that mean?

DONNA/BONNIE
It looks you don't understand how things work.
(Gets up)
It's all about give and take.

REGGIE/BRENDA
I understand perfectly and I don't want to give this
director what he wants to take. This guy is notorious for
his exploits with his actresses. Sure they get famous for a
movie or two but then he moves on to the next one and
the old one fades into nothing.

DONNA/BONNIE
It looks like this was a mistake...

REGGIE/BRENDA
Sorry to waste your time.

DONNA/BONNIE
Well, maybe Morality Movie Studio is looking for actresses.
Oh, wait. There's no such thing.

(DONNA/BONNIE exits)

REGGIE/BRENDA
(To self)
Wow, Madame Mooch. You sure were right about this one.

MACY/HEATHER
(Returns)
Was that the cast agent? Wow, she sure didn't look happy.
What happened?

REGGIE/BRENDA
I just blew my chance at fame and fortune.

MACY/HEATHER
Why'd you do that?

REGGIE/BRENDA
Because I'm an idiot. What are you doing back here?

MACY/HEATHER
Dan called and canceled our dinner date so I went and
bought a lottery ticket. I used Madame Mooch's numbers.

REGGIE/BRENDA
That was a waste of a dollar.

MACY/HEATHER
It was worth a try.

REGGIE/BRENDA
Let's go, okay?

(12006 enters with a gun that's very obviously a toy)

12006/JO
Where's Mooch?

REGGIE/BRENDA
She's in her secret room laughing at us no doubt.
(Tries to go as does MACY/HEATHER)
Can we get by please?

(12006 moves to block REGGIE/BRENDA and MACY/HEATHER)

12006/JO
Where's Mooch?

REGGIE/BRENDA
All you have to do is wave a few dollars around. She'll appear.
(Falls out of character)

12006/JO
(Holds up gun)
Where's Mooch?

MACY/HEATHER
She's got a gun!

REGGIE/BRENDA
Hey, now lady. We don't want any trouble.

12006
Where's Mooch?

REGGIE/BRENDA
I don't know what your problem with her is, but it has nothing to do with us. So if we could just go...

(12006 pushes MACY into a chair but REGGIE avoids 12006 this time and sits on her own)

MACY
Ow.

REGGIE/BRENDA
You know what? No crime has been committed. As far as I can tell, you have a permit for that gun. No crime. No problem. Let's go, Heather.

(They start to get up and 12006/JO pushes REGGIE/BRENDA down)

REGGIE/BRENDA
Ow.

(MELINDA/MOOCH enters)

MELINDA/MOOCH
Hello, Jo. What do you want?
(12006/JO looks around nervously)
Are you upset about what I said to your husband?

(12006/JO freezes. REGGIE/BRENDA gets up and nods her head for her. The followings lines need to have the feel that they are improvising since 12006/JO isn't saying her lines)

MACY/HEATHER
What did you say to her husband?

MELINDA/MOOCH
I said she was sleeping around.

(They pause a second but nothing from 12006/JO)

MACY/HEATHER
So Jo? Were you sleeping around?

(REGGIE makes 12006's head shake no)

MELINDA/MOOCH
Oh, dear.

MACY/HEATHER
(Getting agry for 12006/JO)
"Oh, dear." Is that all you can say?! You ruined her life and you just say, "Oh, dear."

REGGIE/BRENDA
I can't believe your husband would leave you based on something some two-bit psychic would say.

MELINDA/MOOCH
How dare you call me a…

(12006/JO comes to life and shoves gun at MELINDA/MOOCH. This makes them all jump)

12006/JO
Shut up, Mooch.
(Holds gun up to MOOCH's head)
So psychic lady, can you see what's in your future?

MELINDA/MOOCH
Sorry, I can't predict the future for myself.

12006/JO
I can tell you now your future will be a short one.
(Pulls trigger. Click. No bullets. MOOCH faints. MACY screams)
Where'd I put my gun clip?

REGGIE/BRENDA
Run, Heather!
(REGGIE pulls MACY toward door)

MACY/HEATHER
What about Mooch?

REGGIE/BRENDA
We'll call the cops.

12006/JO
(Finds clip and puts it in gun. Points it at them just as they get to the door)
Hold it!

(REGGIE and MACY freeze)

REGGIE/BRENDA
I think she found her bullets.

MACY/HEATHER
We're gonna die.

12006/JO
Sit down.

MACY/HEATHER
(Sees flashing lights out window)
I think we have a problem.

12006/JO
Who called the cops?

REGGIE/BRENDA
We didn't. You know maybe you better surrender. You didn't do anything yet.

MELINDA/MOOCH
(Wakes up)
Am I still alive or has someone summoned my spirit?

REGGIE/BRENDA
Unfortunately you're still among the living.

(REGGIE and MACY help MELINDA up)

MELINDA/MOOCH
I see the police have arrived.

REGGIE/BRENDA
Give yourself up. It's the only way.

MACY/HEATHER
(Looks to window)
Now I think there's a news crew.

MELINDA/MOOCH
All this free publicity will be good for business.

MACY/HEATER
Hey, let's see if we get on TV.

REGGIE/BRENDA
You're way too excited about this, Heather.

(MOOCH goes to TV and turns it on)

REPORTER (Voice)
We're live outside Madame Moose's shop...

MOOCH
Mooch not Moose.

12006/JO
I like Moose better.

REPORTER
(Recorded voice or DONNA on microphone)
The police say the suspect is armed and dangerous.

MACY/HEATHER
That doesn't sound good.

REGGIE/BRENDA
Hey! Maybe if you go on the news and tell them your story and let everyone know what a big fraud she is.

MELINDA/MOOCH
Can't you shoot me in the foot and run. That would be much better for business.

12006/JO
How about I shoot you in the foot AND talk to the reporter.

MACY/HEATHER
Shhh. Wait. They have the lottery numbers at the bottom of the screen.

REGGIE/BRENDA
Heather. Can't that wait?

MACY/HEATHER
Three! I've got a three.

REGGIE/BRENDA
Heather... please... not...

MACY/HEATHER
Five! Got a five!

REGGIE/BRENDA
Heather...

MACY/HEATHER
Nine! We've got three numbers.

MELINDA/MOOCH
Really? I'm mean, of course.

MACY/HEATHER
Twenty-five! We're winning!

REGGIE/BRENDA
(Getting into it)
Twenty-five. We have twenty-five. Come on 49!

MACY/HEATHER
49!

REGGIE/BRENDA
And the Powerball is...

MACY/HEATHER
Seven! We won!

MELINDA/MOOCH
I told you so.

REGGIE/BRENDA
We won! We won!

(Dances around with MACY. REGGIE and MACY are still jumping up and down. 12006 looks at her gun. Looks at them. MELINDA stops them and points to 12006 who points her gun at them)

12006/JO
So how much did you win?

(REGGIE/BRENDA quickly realized their mistake)

REGGIE/BRENDA
Not much.

(MACY/HEATHER is clueless)

MACY/HEATHER
Only 95 million.

12006/JO
95 million! Dollars?

MELINDA/MOOCH
No, Powerballs.

12006/JO
Shut up!
(Smiles)
This changes everything.
(Points gun and holds out hand)
Hand over the ticket.

(MELINDA sneaks around behind her)

REGGIE/BRENDA
Easy come... easy go.

MACY/HEATHER
No...

REGGIE/BRENDA
No, what?

MACY/HEATHER
No, I'm not giving her our ticket. This is our ticket.

REGGIE/BRENDA
Heather, this is no time to get a backbone.

MACY/HEATHER
But we won it. It's ours.

REGGIE/BRENDA
(Shrugs and smiles sheepishly at 12006)
It's amazing what a few million can do to a person.

12006/JO
Hand it over or I'll take it off your dead body.

MOOCH
(Picks up crystal ball and moves behind 12006)
Oh, Jo?!
(12006 turns and MELINDA smashes it on her head)
She didn't see that coming.
(12006 falls to the ground and passes out)
So what do you girls say to sharing that ticket?

MACY/HEATHER
Sure! I think I could spare a million or two.

REGGIE/BRENDA
It's the least we could do. I assume there's a "we" in this deal.

MACY/HEATHER
Of course, I wouldn't have bought this if hadn't asked Mooch for the numbers.

REGGIE/BRENDA
I have to ask you, Mooch, do you always picking winning numbers?

MELINDA/MOOCH
Never. I got lucky this time.

REGGIE/BRENDA
What a story. Those reporters will be all over us.

MACY/HEATHER
We'll be famous.

(GUS rushes in and stops and points his gun)

GUS
Everybody freeze!

(Lights fade to black. Audience applauds and MELINDA is on stage bowing and waving. CAPTAIN brings her flowers)

CAPTAIN
Stunning performance, Melinda.

MELINDA
I aim to please.

CAPTAIN
Thank you everyone for coming tonight. We'll have a photo session with Ms. Street shortly. Also time for questions from reporters.

MELINDA
I always have time for my fans too.

CAPTAIN
Where are the others?

MELINDA
They must not have wanted to steal my moment in the sun.

CAPTAIN
That doesn't sound like them.
(On radio)
Gus, you there? Where are the rest of the ladies?

MELINDA
They usually go behind the beaded curtain.

(CAPTAIN goes to beaded curtain and moves it. Wall is there)

CAPTAIN
What's going on? How do you open this thing?

MELINDA
I'm not sure.

CAPTAIN
Open up in there!
(On radio)
Security. Get in here. We have a problem.
(Security guard enters. It's actually DONNA)
Take Ms. Street to her dressing room and keep her there. Tell the other guards to secure the building.
(DONNA exits with MELINDA. CAPTAIN figures out how to open door)
Got it.

(Door opens and GUS is tied to a chair with MACY on top of him kissing him. When they audience can see them, MACY jumps off)

MACY
It was horrible Captain. They tied up Gus and ran for it.

CAPTAIN
(On radio)
I need backup!

(CAPTAIN runs off stage and MACY smiles at GUS who smiles back and she closes false door. Two security guards rush in. It's REGGIE and 12006)

REGGIE
I wonder where they went?
(12006 shrugs and smiles)
Hey, there's one of them.

(12006 and REGGIE rush into audience and grabs audience member)

REGGIE (CONT.)
Trying to escape huh? Well, we'll just have to see about that.
(Audience member protests)
You're not a prisoner? Let me see some ID.
(Gets wallet from purse)
I'll just keep this wallet for evidence purposes.
(Gets keys)
And your car keys. Which car is yours? We'll need to investigate it too. Make sure there aren't any criminals stashed in the trunk. And we'll check for drugs too. See her eyes. She looks like an addict. Take her away!

(12006 grabs audience member and REGGIE follows smiling)

END OF PLAY

ADAPTED MONOLOGUES

"MELINDA STREET"

Monologue #1 - approximately 30 seconds

MELINDA

Mind if I step out for a bit, Officer?
Just for a second. I promise I'll be right back.
Oh, what's the mater, Officer? Am I getting a little too close.
Oh, I'm so scared. Little police man's gonna handcuff me.
Or is that a game you like to play with the girls?

END OF MONOLOGUE 1

"MELINDA STREET"

Monologue #2 - approximately 1 minute

MELINDA

Look, ladies. If you want to act with me you've got to follow a few simple rules. When I'm on stage, you all back up and give me room. The key is to stay upstage of me at all times.

(Points upstage)

That's upstage. And I will be downstage.

(She wakes downstage regally)

Who is the professional award winning actor here? Me. So let me handle this. The key, girls, is to not steal my light. You'll have your time to play act while I'm off stage.

(reacts to one of the other women and speaks mockingly)

But... But... Nothing. That's the way it's going to be.

END OF MONOLOGUE 2

"IN FOR MURDER"

GUS
If I tell you what she's in prison for, then you won't say anything to the Captain?

(Waits for reply and then nods)

Fine. She's a red shirt. She's in for murder.

(Likes the reaction he gets so he plays it up)

She was in this murder mystery on Broadway and she killed the entire cast. For real. And nobody knew it until the play was over. I mean like all the actors were supposed to pretend to die but she really was killing them. They don't know why she did it either. She didn't even go for an insanity plea. She was calm and collected in the trial. And she checked out fine on all the tests for mental stability. And now she's going to be acting in a play with all of you...

END OF MONOLOGUE

"BETTER WORLD TOMORROW"

CAPTAIN
Well, you're gonna make it work. The warden got the money for this project and he's not giving the money back. And with a big name like Ms. Street involved, this will bring a lot of much needed media attention for the warden. The warden is publishing a book and we hope to have this little play ready for the day it hits the bookstores. He had some writer come in and help him but it's his book. It's his plan for reforming the entire prison system in our country. He gave me an advance copy. It's called "More Prisons Today, A Better World Tomorrow."

END OF MONOLOGUE

"ICE QUEEN"

MACY

Is she playing an ice queen with a stick up her butt?

I don't understand why she doesn't like me. What have I done to her? I mean I practically worship her and all she does is throw insults at me and trashes my presents.

Well, I've written her a letter almost every day since she's been here and she hasn't written back. In fact she trashes my letters.

I know because I go through her trash.

And I made her these little pictures with me and her doing things together like going to movie premieres and going to the beach...

I cut pictures out of magazines of her and take photos of me and put them together. I sometimes put my head on pictures of Pamela Anderson when I can find them because we have real similar figures.

But she ripped up the last picture I made right in front of me. I swear I'm going to resign as the president of her fan club.

END OF MONOLOGUE

"PLAN B"

MACY
You could drop one of those theatre lights up there on her. Those guards would sure scramble then.

We'll call that plan B.

You sure we can't drop that on her just for fun?

I guess I don't want to become a red shirt... red's not my color.

What's the point of escaping? My time is almost up and if I ran Gussie and I couldn't...

...Gussie made me promise not to tell anyone about his proposal...

I just realized that I can't even shop for my own ring. Parole violation.

And I hate shopping online.
Online, catalogs... that's like pure torture... I have to touch diamonds. See them sparkle.

I saw this wedding dress once that sparkled like diamonds. It was an outdoor wedding and the sun lit her up... Oh, it was the most beautiful thing I've ever seen. I need that dress!

And they can play my favorite song at wedding as I am walking like a giant diamond to Gus...

(MACY is lost in some fantasy and starts singing)

"Diamonds are a girls... best... friend..."

(MACY snaps out of it)

Please don't tell him I told you.

END OF MONOLOGUE

"RADIANT TALENT"

BRENDA

That local theatre reviewer is an idiot. He wouldn't know a play if a stage fell on him.

(Looks at review in newspaper)

Wait. This review is really good.

(Reads)

"Brenda Star lives up to her name. Her radiant talent brightens this otherwise ordinary play."

(Takes paper)

This is so great! My agent will go nuts. We better go get a copy of the paper so I can show my agent. Wait a minute. This smells like a set up. Wasn't that awfully good timing? Madame Mooch says I'm going to be famous and then this person comes in here and acts like I'm some new star.

(Pauses and listens to her friend)

You're right. How could she fake that newspaper review? It's a coincidence. That's all.

(Cell phone rings)

Hello? Hi, Gina.

(To friend)

It's my agent. I'll bet she saw the review.

BRENDA (CONT.)

(To Phone)

Yeah, I read it.

(Pause)

Very good.

(Shocked)

What?

(Pause)

No way.

(Waves away friend who is trying to talk to her)

Shhhh.

(To phone)

Sorry, my friend is talking to me.

(Pause)

Yes, let's do it.

(Looks around)

I hate to admit this, but I'm at some psychic reading place.

(Picks up brochure)

BRENDA (CONT.)

Madame Mooch...

(Pause)

You know her?

(To friend)

My agent's been here.

(Pause)

Sure I'll wait for her here.

(Hangs up phone)

You won't believe this. Somebody is filming a movie in town and they saw my show last night. They want me to be in their movie. Gina said there are some big stars in it too. One of them had a scheduling conflict and can't come. Gina's sending the casting director over to see me now. They need somebody immediately and want me to do it.

(Stops)

This can't be happening. Where is that Madame Money? Come out, Madame! I want a word with you. I know how these stories go. Remember that story the Monkey's Paw? At first, everything is great. You get everything you wish for, then the bottom drops out. Don't be mad, Heather. I'm sorry. I have to admit there might be something beyond my comprehension going on here.

BRENDA (CONT.)

(Calls out)

Madame Mooch. I need a word with you. I wonder why she isn't reappearing?

(Pulls out money)

I'm not speaking her language.

(Waves bill)

I have something green for you.

END OF MONOLOGUE

"TRYING TO ESCAPE"

(This monologue is best performed when the actor can interact with the audience and use an audience member or another person to interact with)

REGGIE
I wonder where they went? Hey, there's one of them.

(REGGIE rushes into audience and grabs audience member)

Trying to escape huh? Well, we'll just have to see about that.

(Audience member protests)

You're not a prisoner? Let me see some ID.

(Gets wallet from purse)

I'll just keep this wallet for evidence purposes.

(Gets keys)

And your car keys. Which car is yours? We'll need to investigate it too. Make sure there aren't any criminals stashed in the trunk. And we'll check for drugs too. See her eyes. She looks like an addict. Take her away!

END OF MONOLOGUE

Printed in Great Britain
by Amazon